Welcome to the galaxy of Queensland Year 3 handwriting!

Hello, my name is Sirius, and I am the brightest star in the night sky! I'm here to help you along the way ... in a *Sirius* kind of way!

My ticket to the Moon

Name: ____________________

Age: __________ Class: __________

Birthday: ____________________

Teacher: ____________________

My progress passport

You are travelling on a spaceship expedition around the galaxy. Colour in the circles as you progress through the book.

Aa

I can print.

I can write a head, body and tail letter.

I remember to retrace for horizontal joins to anti-clockwise letters.

I can do drop-in joins.

I can connect drop-in joins to a, c, d, g and q.

I can retrace horizontal joins to tall letters.

I can do horizontal joins to double letters.

I can do horizontal joins.

al

I can write letters with exit flicks.

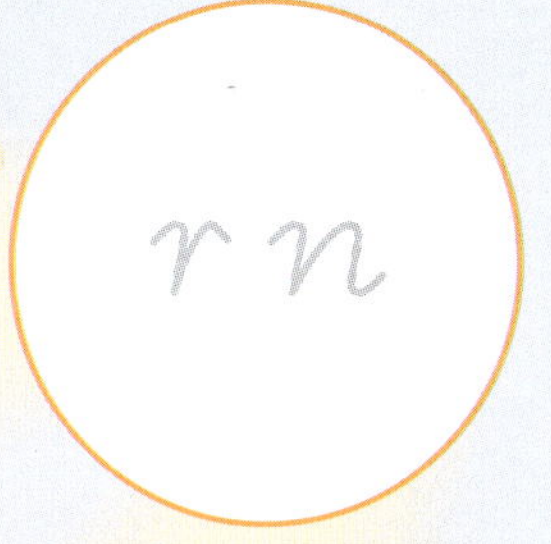

rn

I know the letters m, n, r and x have rounded entries.

ij

I know the letters i, j, p, u, v, w and y have pointed entries.

m

I can write letters with entry flicks.

hi

I can do diagonal joins.

Blast off!

I can write fluently and legibly.

AB

I remember capital letters do not join.

bg

I know the letters b, g, j, p, s, y and z do not join.

if

I can do the loopy f.

Before you begin writing ...

Here are the **3Ps** that will help you with your writing: **p**osture, **p**encil grip and **p**aper position. You will be reminded about these as you go through the book.

Posture

Relax your arms and make sure the chair supports your back. Put your feet flat on the floor.

Pencil grip

One of the most important decisions you can make is how you hold your pencil. Hold your pencil firmly between your thumb and index finger, balanced on your middle finger. (Your grip should be 2.5 centimetres before the end of the pencil. Don't grip too tightly!)

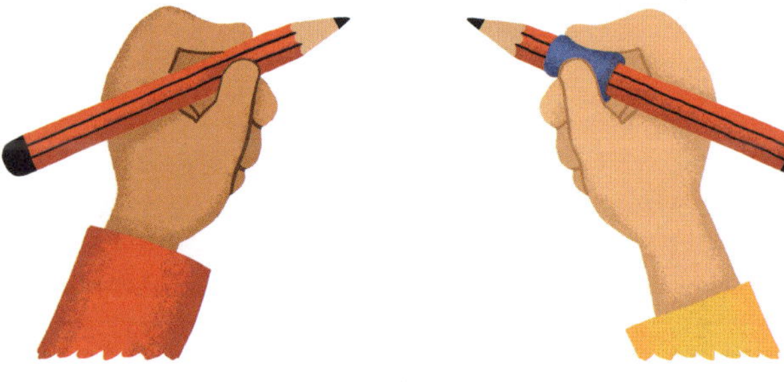

Left-handed Right-handed

Paper position

Angle your page and use your non-writing hand to steady the page.

Left-handed

Right-handed

Left-handers may form some letters differently. For example, for the capital letters A, E, F, H and T, the left-handed person might go from right to left to make the join.

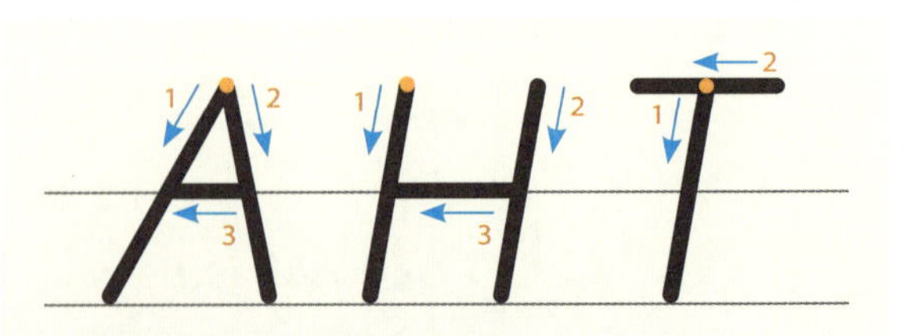

Queensland Beginner's print

Printing letters

Learning intention:
To revise my print handwriting

Trace and print these lower-case and capital letters.

aA bB cC dD eE fF gG

hH iI jJ kK lL mM nN

oO pP qQ rR sS tT uU

vV wW xX yY zZ

From the alphabet above, find and print all the tall lower-case letters that touch the top orange line.

above
on
below

f h

Find and print all the short lower-case letters.

above
on
below

a c

above
on
below

Find and print all the tail lower-case letters.

above
on
below

g j

Printing numerals

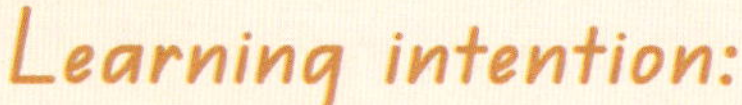

Learning intention:
To revise my printing of numerals and punctuation

Trace and copy these numerals

Printing punctuation

Trace and then copy these punctuation marks on the lines below.

. . . , , , : : : ; ; ;

' ' ' " " " " ? ? ? ! ! ! / / /

Self-assessment Draw a star beside your top three numerals.

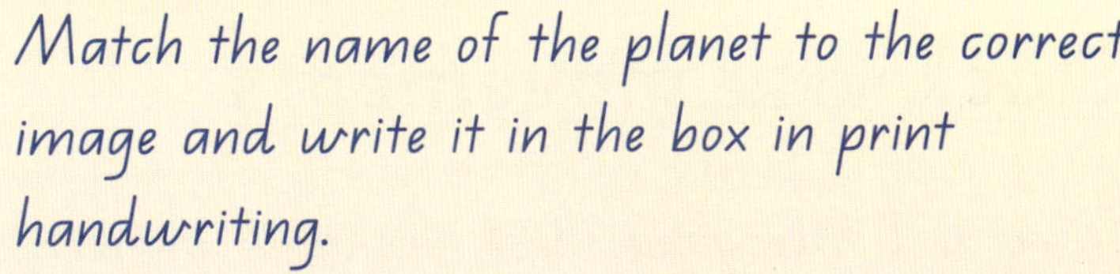

Printing names

Learning intention:
To label diagrams using print handwriting

Tip! When we label maps and diagrams, we use print handwriting.

Neptune Saturn
Venus Uranus
Mars Earth
Jupiter Mercury

Match the name of the planet to the correct image and write it in the box in print handwriting.

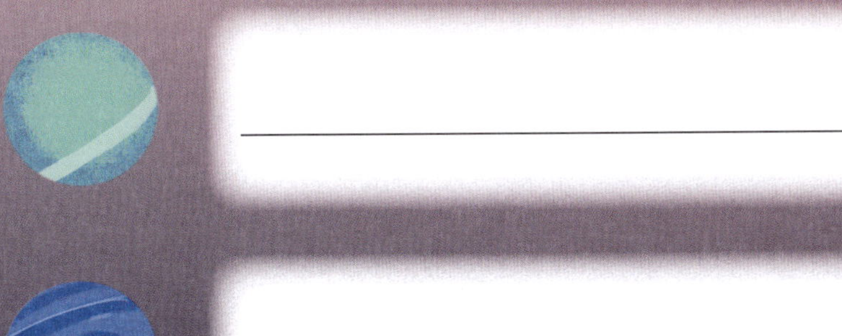

"My Very Educated Mother Just Served Us Noodles"

Direction of movement

Learning intention: To practise letters with clockwise movements

Clockwise movements

Trace and then copy these clockwise patterns.

Trace and then copy these clockwise letters.

Complete the numbers on the clock. Then complete the grey line around the clock and add an arrow to show which way is clockwise.

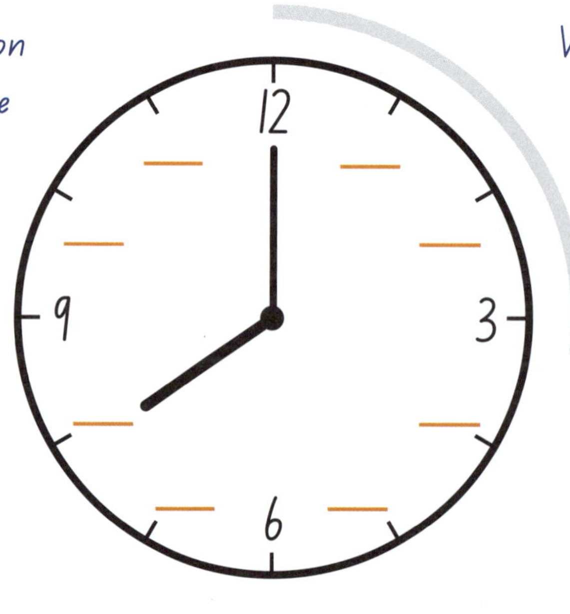

What time is showing on this clock?

DID YOU KNOW ... that a day on Saturn is only 11 hours?

Anti-clockwise movements

Learning intention:
To practise letters with anti-clockwise movements

Trace and then copy these anti-clockwise patterns.

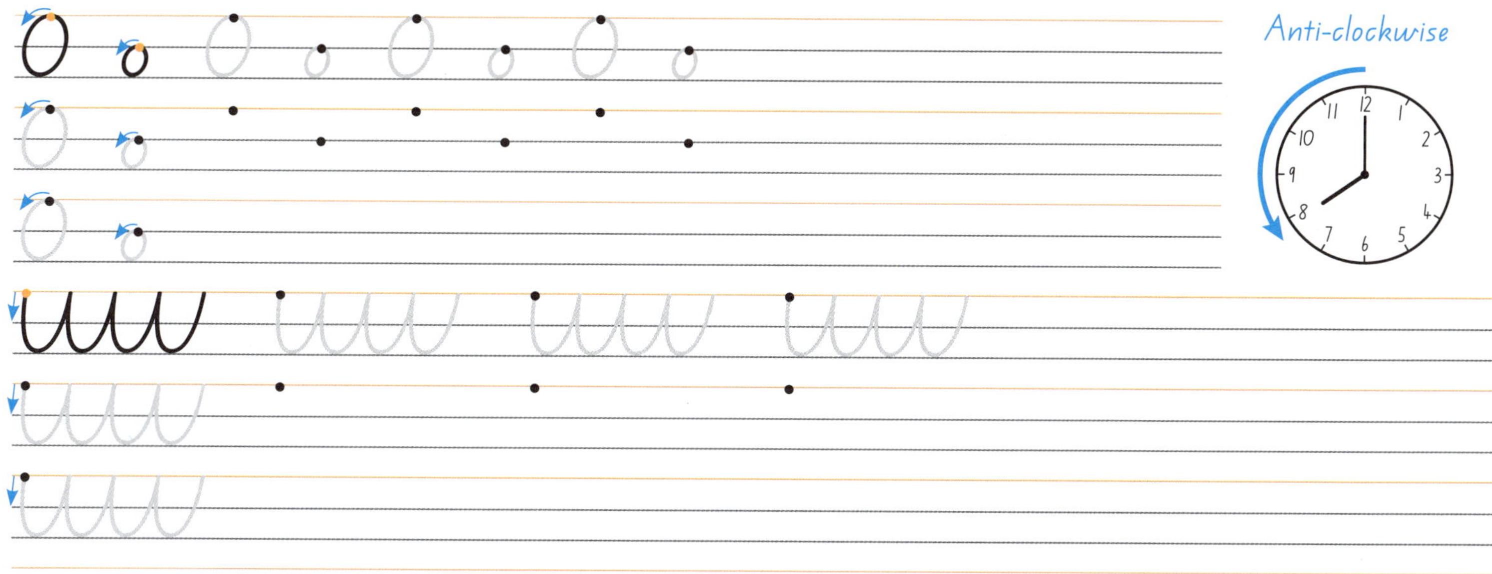

Trace and then copy the anti-clockwise letters.

a c d e f

g o q s

u v w y

Write each anti-clockwise letter in the correct column. Write its capital letter next to it.

Short letters	Tall and tail letters
aA	gG

Downstroke and straight-line patterns

Learning intention:
To practise letters that have a straight line

Trace and then copy these downstroke movements.

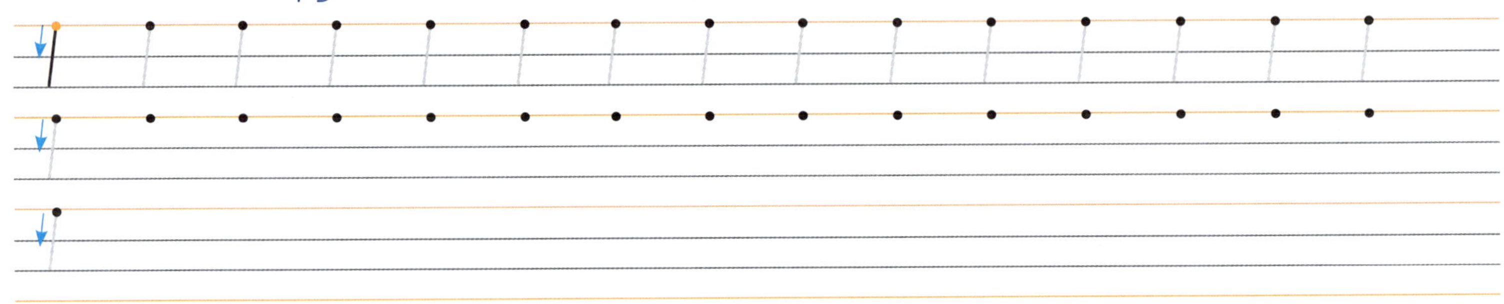

Trace and then copy these horizontal movements.

Trace and then copy these downstroke letters.

l lit i ill
t till h hit
j jelly f fill

Diagonal letters

Learning intention:
To practise letters that have a diagonal

Trace and then copy these diagonal movements. Start at the dot.

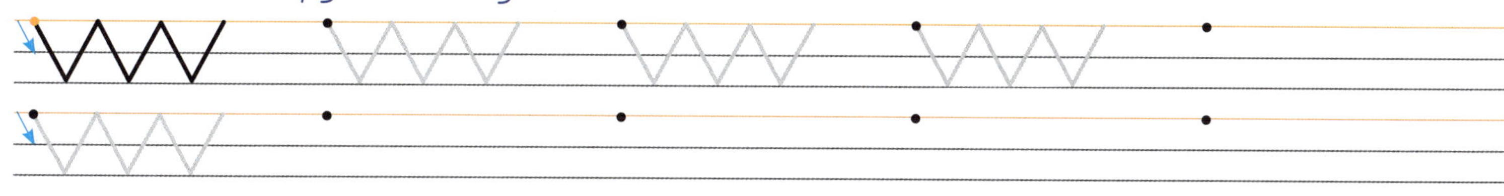

Trace and then copy these combined movements.

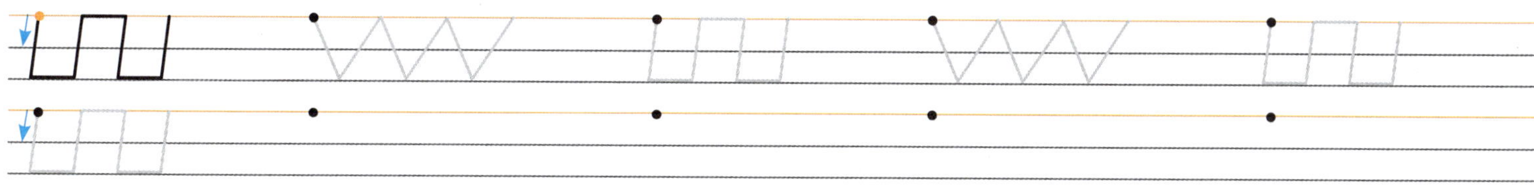

Trace and then copy these diagonal capital letters and their lower-case letters.

Trace the diagonal track of the shooting stars, using the dot as a starting point.

Consolidating

Learning intention: To practise more patterns before writing

Trace and then copy.

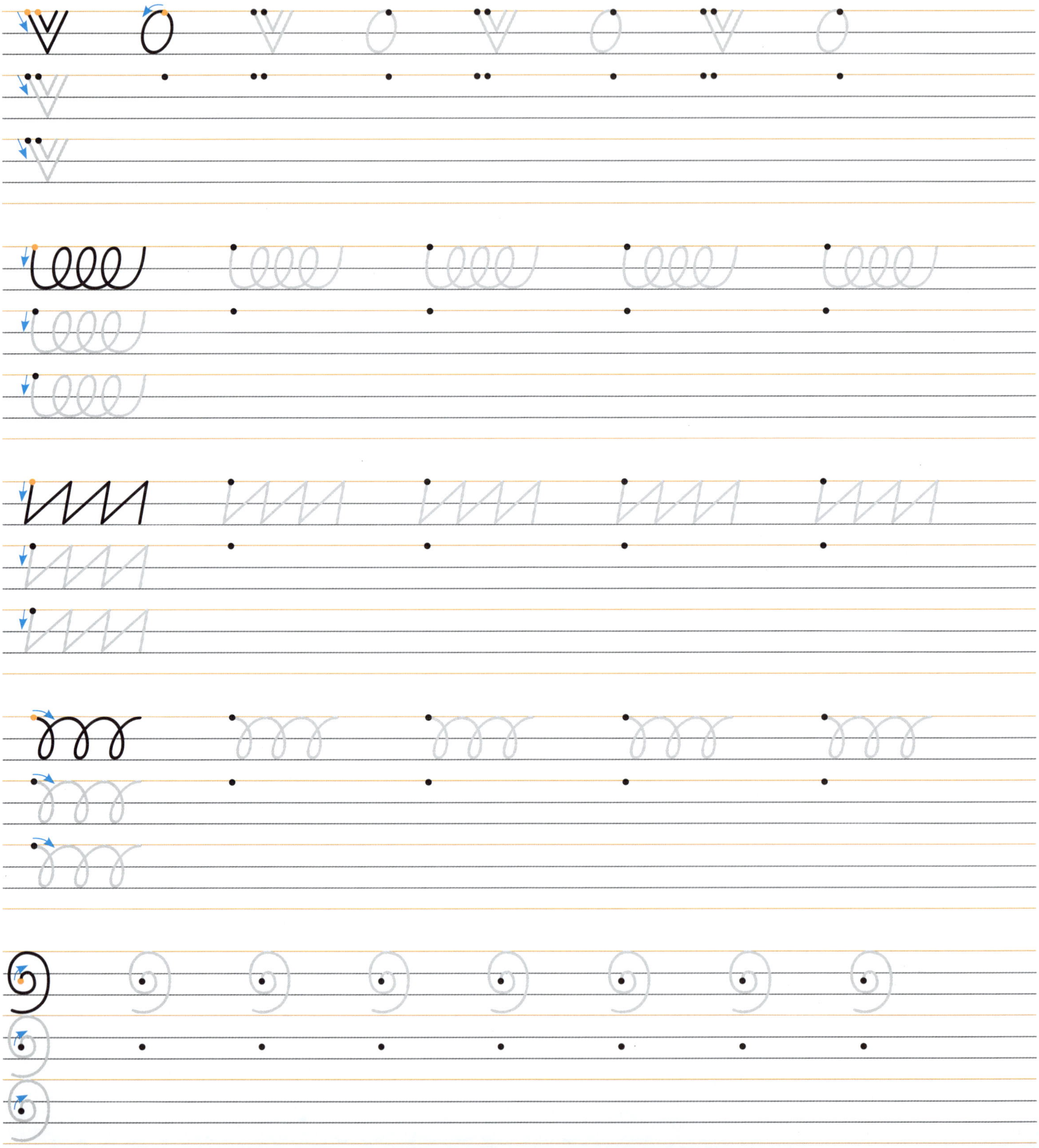

Assessment: Print handwriting

Learning intention:

To combine all movements and write in print handwriting

Write all the capital and lower-case letters of the alphabet in print handwriting.

Aa Bb

Copy the following in print handwriting.

A day on Mercury is 1408 hours and on

A

Venus it is 5832 hours. A day on Earth

V

is 24 hours and on Mars it is 25 hours.

i

Jupiter has the shortest day: only 10 hours.

J

Self-assessment of print handwriting:

Congratulations! You have completed the revision of print handwriting. Colour in your progress on page 2.

- ❑ I need more confidence
- ❑ I understand but need practice
- ❑ Over the Moon!

Teacher comment

Passport

Exit flicks

Revising exit flicks

Learning intention:

To add exit flicks to help get from one letter to another

Tip! Exit flicks help you join letters in a word.

Trace these letters and words. Add the missing letters to complete the word.
Note! One of these words is a proper noun and will need a capital letter.

a a a	___ steroids
c c c	___ omet
d d d	___ warf planet
e e e	___ clips ___
h h h	green ___ ouse
i i i	Jup ___ ter
k k k	___ uiper belt
l l l	techno ___ ogy
m m m	___ eteor
n n n	super ___ ova
t t t	___ elescope
u u u	Sat ___ rn
v v v	gra ___ ity
w w w	___ hited ___ arf
x x x	e ___ ploration

Practising exit flicks

Learning intention: To practise exit flicks

I am successful when I can:

- ❑ check my 3Ps
- ❑ make my exit flick smooth rather than pointy.

Trace and then copy.

Asteroids are rocky objects left over

from when our solar system formed

4.6 billion years ago. There are millions

of asteroids. Most asteroids are located

in the asteroid belt, between

Mars and Jupiter.

Self-assessment Draw a star above three of your smoothest exit flicks.

Letters without exit flicks

Learning intention: To understand that capital letters do not contain exit flicks

Capital letters do not have an exit flick because they don't join to other letters.

Trace and then copy.

Claudia and Ali went on a mission to

Jupiter, the fifth planet from the Sun.

They also visited Mars, Saturn, Uranus

and Neptune on their mission.

They saw moons, many

different-sized asteroids and

comets with long tails.

The letter f

Learning intention:

To practise writing the letter f below the baseline

Tip!

Remember that the letter f has a tail below the baseline and the crossbar is angled to make it easier to join to the next letter.

Trace these letters.

f f f f f f f f

Trace and then copy these words.

full face fine family flexible

friends fire find first factor

focus fusion floor fraction fabric

fun five few four

fix fork fantastic

Consolidating

Trace and then copy.

Sirius and Juliette loved travelling to

space in a rocket. The absence of gravity

made them feel as light as a feather.

It was like floating through a mystical,

untouched world. (Gravity is a force

that holds you to Earth's surface.)

For years it was believed that Earth was

the only planet in our solar system with

liquid water. Recently, NASA revealed

that there is intermittent running

water on Mars too. Space exploration

increases scientific research and technology

developments. It also helps us to appreciate

the beauty of life on Earth. Sirius and

Juliette were amazed to learn that there

are more stars in the universe than grains

of sand on all the beaches on Earth.

Draw a star above three of your smoothest exit flicks.

Assessment: Exit flicks

Trace and then copy these letters with exit flicks.

a a c c d d e e

f f h h i i k k

l l m m n n r r

t t u u v v w w x x

Practise writing these words with exit flicks.

Aurora Earth planets galaxy

asteroid gravity Neptune

Congratulations! You've completed the revision of exit flicks.

Colour in your progress on page 3.

❑ I need more confidence ❑ I understand but need practice ❑ Over the Moon!

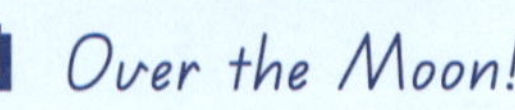

Teacher comment

Entry flicks

Revising entry flicks

What is an entry flick?

Tip!

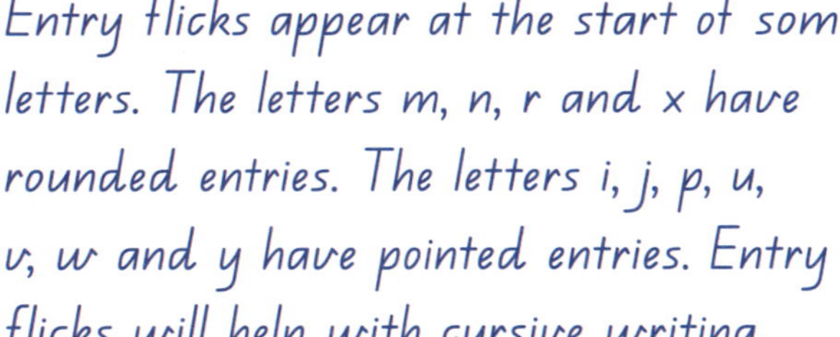

Entry flicks appear at the start of some letters. The letters m, n, r and x have rounded entries. The letters i, j, p, u, v, w and y have pointed entries. Entry flicks will help with cursive writing.

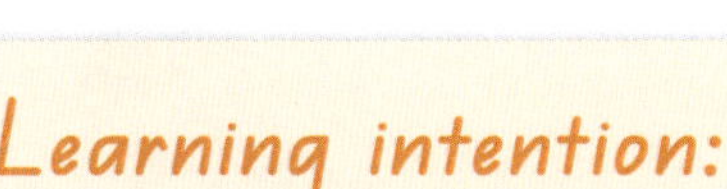

Learning intention:

To write letters with a rounded entry flick

Trace and then copy these letters with rounded entry flicks.

m n r x m n r x

Trace these letters and words with entry and exit flicks. Then add the letter to complete the word.

m m m	co_et
n n n	u_iverse
r r r	c_aters
x x x	e_traterrestrial

Trace and then copy these sentences.

The moons near Neptune move in amazing motions. Radiant rings surround Saturn.

Exotic stars explode in galaxies.

Practising entry flicks

Learning intention:
To write letters with a pointed entry flick

Trace these letters. Then circle the letters that have entry flicks.

a b c d e f g h
i j k l m n o p
q r s t u v w x
y z

Trace these letters with pointed entry flicks, then write each one ten times.

i
j
p
u
v
w
y

I am successful when I can:

- ❑ sit with my back straight
- ❑ hold the pencil correctly
- ❑ position my paper
- ❑ make my entry flick smooth.

OXFORD UNIVERSITY PRESS

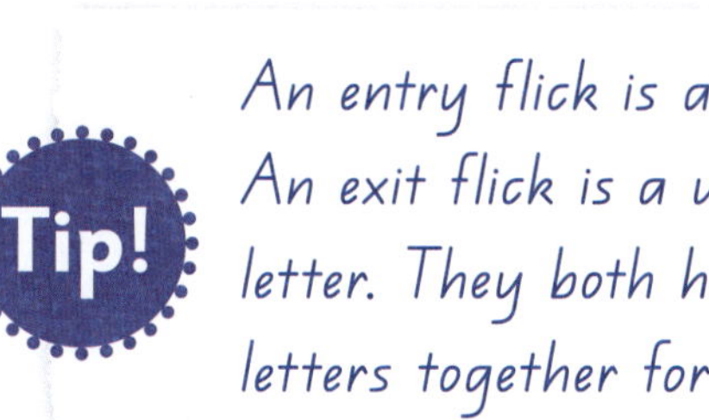

Tip! An entry flick is a way into a letter. An exit flick is a way out of a letter. They both help when you join letters together for cursive writing.

Trace and then copy the words below.

change pattern time natural

human actions erosion source

energy axis night season

orbit day galaxy dwarf planet

generate nocturnal hover gaze

function gases satellite fuel void

Circle your neatest word and add a tick above three of your best entry flicks.

Letters without entry flicks

Learning intention:
To understand that capital letters do not have entry flicks

Capital letters do not have entry flicks because they don't join to other letters in the word.

Trace this text. Circle the capital letters when you have finished.

Alessia read a book from her school library that stated: "In 1969, Neil Armstrong became the first astronaut to walk on the Moon".

Then she taught her younger sister, Daniela, all the names of the planets in the solar system: Mercury, Venus, Earth, Mars, Jupiter, Saturn, Uranus and Neptune.

That night, they looked up at the Moon and marvelled that people had travelled that far through space.

I am successful when I can:
- [ ] check my 3Ps
- [ ] make my entry flick smooth.

OXFORD UNIVERSITY PRESS

Consolidating

Learning intention:
To practise writing letters with entry flicks

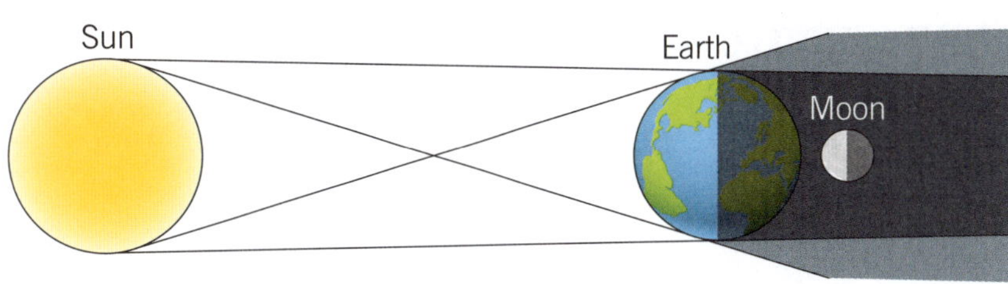

The Earth rotates on its axis every 24 hours, which makes day and night.

Trace and then copy the following text.

The Sun is a major source of energy that
warms our planet. It takes the Earth and
Moon 365 days (one year) to orbit the Sun.
Gravity from the Moon pulls on the Earth
and causes waves in the ocean. Like Earth,
the Moon has a day side and a night side.
Can you see the daytime Moon today?

We can only sometimes see the Moon during the day. This depends on the moon phase.

Assessment: Entry flicks

I am successful when I can:

- ❑ sit with my back straight
- ❑ hold my pencil correctly
- ❑ position my paper
- ❑ make my entry flick smooth.

Trace and then copy these letters with entry flicks.

i j p m n r u v y

Write four words that contain at least one entry flick.

Trace and then copy this text.

Ravi the astronaut flew to space in a rocket to study weightlessness.

Self-assessment of entry flicks:

Congratulations! You've completed the revision of entry flicks. Colour in your progress on page 3.

❑ I need more confidence ❑ I understand but need practice ❑ Over the Moon!

Passport

Teacher comment

Diagonal joins

Learning intention:
To write letters with a diagonal join

Introducing diagonal joins

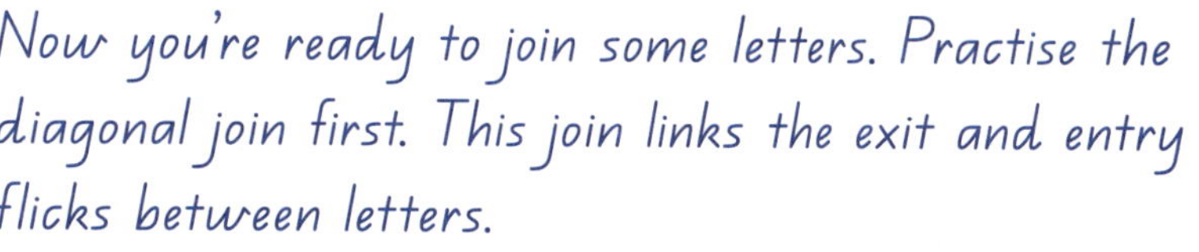

Now you're ready to join some letters. Practise the diagonal join first. This join links the exit and entry flicks between letters.

Practise the diagonal join between h and i.

hi hi hi hi

Trace and then copy these diagonal joins.

ai an ap ce cu cy

de di dy em ei ey

he hi hu in le tr

as es ns

The letter s changes after a diagonal join. Trace and then copy these diagonal joins to s.

as es is ls ns ms ts

Practising diagonal joins

Can you continue the pattern from the starting point without lifting your pencil?

Learning intention:
To connect letters with a diagonal join

uuuu • uuuu • • • •

uuuu • uuuu • • • •

Trace and then copy these diagonal joins to rounded entries. The first one is done for you.

ie — am an ie im in ip ir

am

ke — un en ke ki kn kr ky

le — ar er le li lm lu ly

me — ax ix me mi mm mp my

sum nun axe knee pun hum line

bin tin mum Sun mix aim new

ni

45°

The exit flicks go up at an angle of about 45 degrees to join to the next letter.

Trace and then copy these letters and words.

ni ne nn nr nu ny

te ti tn tr tu ty

ue ui um un up uy

my tip in bin he her him

cent win hum sink sip

grin tip scientist save ink

Diagonal joins to tall letters

Learning intention:
To use a diagonal join to tall letters

Without lifting the pencil, you can make a diagonal join with an extended exit flick.

a with an exit flick	a with a diagonal join up	a joined to h
a	a	ah

Trace these diagonal joins to tall letters, and then copy them below. The first one is done for you.

ah ah ah ah al al al al

ah

ak ak ak ak ab ab ab ab

ch ch ch ck ck ck at et ot

ad ad ad el el el ek ek ek

Continue the pattern without lifting your pencil. Then go back and dot each letter i.

ılılı ılılı

this ✓

at

Trace and then copy these letters on the lines below.

at at at at at at at

it it it it it it it

ut ut ut ut et et et et

Let's look at some joins to double letters.

Trace and then copy these letters and names.

nn ee ll tt mm ll tt

Ellie Jannik Alessia Jett Yvette

Billie Arilla Ginni Robbie Bennett

Consolidating

Learning intention: To put diagonal joins into practice

Trace and then copy the following text.

The book "Hidden Figures" is about

three African-American mathematicians

named Mary Jackson, Katherine

Johnson and Dorothy Vaughan. These

women worked for NASA in the

early 1960s. They were very smart and

worked hard. They overcame many

obstacles to contribute to making

early space missions possible.

Assessment: Diagonal joins

Copy these diagonal joins.

ai hu ce im kn ab hi ut

This is how these letters look when they are written with a diagonal join. Trace the letters below and add the diagonal joins. Remember not to lift your pencil!

at

at it hi hu em ie

ke le me ni ke

Copy these words with diagonal joins.

little all aunty bike they then

mine time like humble plane

Self-assessment of diagonal joins:

Congratulations! You have completed your diagonal joins. Colour in your progress on page 3.

❑ I need more confidence

❑ I understand but need practice

❑ Over the Moon!

Teacher comment

Drop-in joins

Introducing drop-in joins

Learning intention:
To write words that contain a drop-in join: a, c, d, g and q

A drop-in join is used when we join to anti-clockwise letters. The exit flick from the first letter reaches high towards the top of the anti-clockwise letter. The anti-clockwise letter is dropped into place.

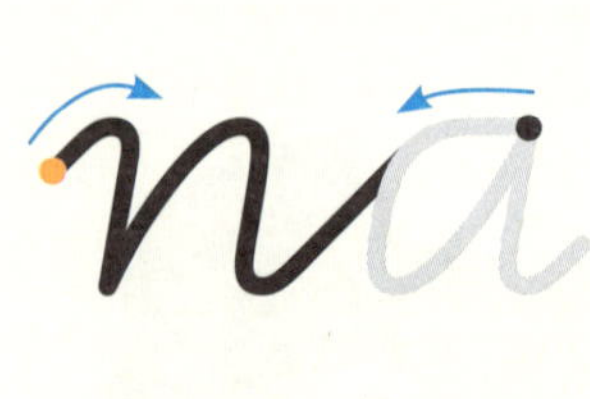

Trace and then copy these drop-in joins.

ma ic ed ng og aq

ca da ea ha ia la na

ec id lc uc ad dd eq

Trace and then copy the dropped-in letters. In another colour, draw a star where the letters meet.

ag dg eg lg ng ug da

a

ca aq eq id iq ta ma

Practising drop-in joins

Learning intention: To join letters with drop-in joins

The dropped-in letter should touch the high exit as it moves down. Make sure there is no gap between the letters (retrace where necessary)!

Trace and then copy these words with drop-in joins.

equate lunar giant name cosmic

fudge unique decade case energy

again stellar astronaut giant boost

Trace and then copy these words with dropped-in letters.

again magma played night

aqua black place jumped

eight equal star titan

match beacon factor matter

Assessment: Drop-in joins

I am successful when I can:

- ❑ check my 3Ps
- ❑ connect my letters in words.

Trace and then copy.

dad had lad mad pad

big dig jig wig zigzag

speck best Tuesday last right

helped mentor blast diameter

Self-assessment of drop-in joins:

Congratulations! You have completed your drop-in joins. Colour in your progress on page 2.

❑ I need more confidence ❑ I understand but need practice ❑ Over the Moon!

Passport

Teacher comment

OXFORD UNIVERSITY PRESS

Horizontal joins

Introducing horizontal joins

Learning intention:
To join letters from short letters

The letters o, r, v and w finish at the top of the letter, so we need to connect these letters with a horizontal join. These letters do not join to the letter e.

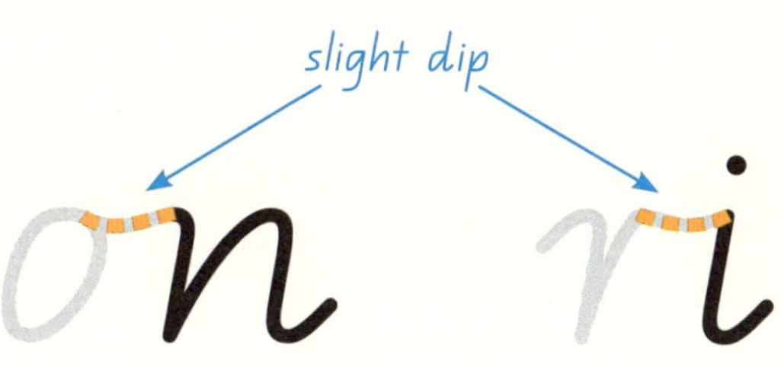

vu wi

Trace and then copy these horizontal joins.

oi om on op or ou ov oy

ri rm rn rp rr ru rv ry

vi vu vv vy vi vu vv vy

wi wu wy wo wp wa wr wc

Continue the fluency pattern.

vuvu vuvu

Practising horizontal joins

Learning intention:
To join letters with horizontal joins

Copy these sentences. Then circle the words that contain a horizontal join.

George and Patrick love to study the

universe. They went to the planetarium

for George's birthday. This morning, they

won an award for writing about asteroids.

Their friends Lea and Jana won a prize

for finding the most constellations when

they were on their school camp.

The letters o and r only need a horizontal join (or exit flick) when they are joining another letter. They do not need an exit flick when they are the last letter in the word.

Horizontal joins to anti-clockwise letters

Learning intention:
To join letters to anti-clockwise letters

retrace section

When making a horizontal join to an anti-clockwise letter, go across to the start of the letter, then retrace.

The orange line shows where the letter is retraced.

Trace and then copy these horizontal joins to anti-clockwise letters.

oa oc oo og os od oa oc oo

ra rc ro rg rs rd ra rc ro

wa wc wo wg ws wd va vo

ocean Saturday good dock

Did you know that Saturday and Saturn were both named after the Roman god of agriculture?

The letter d is the only tall letter that does not start at the top. The horizontal join goes across to the starting point of the letter d.

od

Trace and then copy these words with horizontal joins to anti-clockwise letters.

Today zoo close wrap rocket wooden

revolve roam garden core moons water

Trace these letters. Then, with a coloured pencil, shade in all the squares that have anti-clockwise letter pairs.

oo	tt	pl	xa	hi
ch	ss	og	ck	wc
rm	wo	se	go	os
op	od	fe	wa	ju

No, this is not me giving you a clue that there are 8 anti-clockwise letter pairs!

Write down your own letter pairs showing horizontal joins to the anti-clockwise letters a, c, g, o and s.

OXFORD UNIVERSITY PRESS

Horizontal joins to tall letters

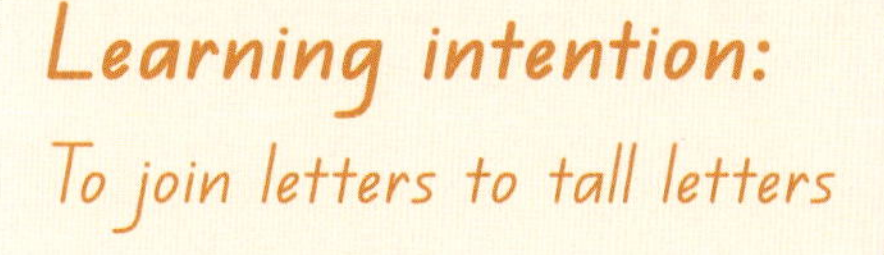

When you make a horizontal join to tall letters, go right to the top and then retrace a little as you move downwards.

Trace these joins to tall letters.

ol rt rk wb wh ok

Trace and then copy.

ol ob oh ot ok

rt rk rh rb wk

wh wt wb vt vh

Trace and then copy these words.

chocolate girl bark stark when

woke solar white verbal orbit

school support evolve growl whole

Horizontal joins with double letters

Learning intention:
To write words with double letters

You can choose whether to join the letter r to the next letter or not.

When we write double letters for r and o, we use a horizontal join. Make sure the double letters are not too far apart.

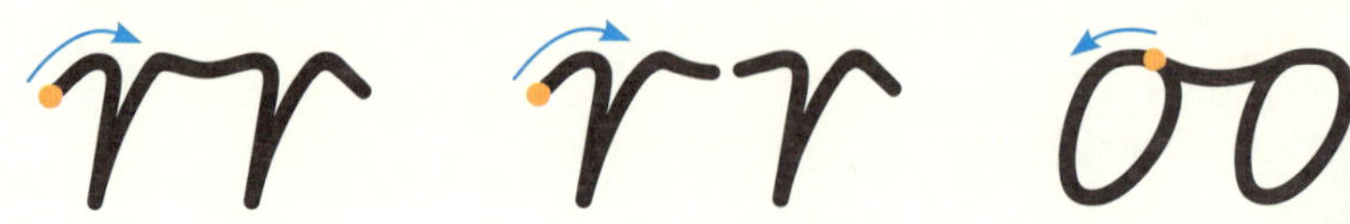

Practise your cursive handwriting by tracing this sentence.

Sirius is good at keeping up with his current studies after school. In the afternoon, he likes reading books and writing. Tomorrow, he has arranged to play sport with a friend.

Consolidating

Learning intention:
To put my horizontal joins into practice

Trace and then copy.

My favourite friend is Finny. She often comes to my house on Sundays. Once, we went to the park with my family on a clear night. We looked through a telescope and saw the Moon and the Southern Cross. It was an amazing night to share with my friend and my family.

Assessment: Horizontal joins

I am successful when I can:

- ❑ check my 3Ps
- ❑ write my letters with horizontal joins.

Copy these words with horizontal joins from o, r, v and w.

open town aware array movie

Copy these words with horizontal joins to anti-clockwise letters.

wait wrong room cosmic rode

Copy these words with horizontal joins to short and tall letters.

start pool solar crater robot

Copy these words with double-letter horizontal joins.

moon irregular extraterrestrial tools

Self-assessment of horizontal joins:

Congratulations! You have completed your horizontal joins. Colour in your progress on page 2.

❑ I need more confidence

❑ I understand but need practice

❑ Over the Moon!

Teacher comment

OXFORD UNIVERSITY PRESS

Tricky joins

Learning intention: To join letters from f

Joins from f

Use the regular f both at the start of a word and after a pencil lift in a word. Use the crossbar to join to the next letter.

Trace and then copy these words to practise your joins from f.

find friend from flight funny

frog fin feel fence fine fire for

five fun fur flag fly joyful

When f joins to an a or o, you need to retrace a little.

Trace and then copy these joins from f to anti-clockwise letters.

fo fa fo fa fo fa fo fa

found favourite family forty

Joins to f

Learning intention: To join to f

When joining to f and ff, the letter f changes to include a loop.

Trace and then copy these joins to f.

of rf wf if

Trace and then copy the following words.

surf define prefix bashful belief

Tip! For double f, the first and second f look the same. They both have loops.

bluff sniff off diff stuff fluff

When you join from a double f, both the letters look the same, but the bar on the second f might sit lower to join to the next letter.

buffer waffle different difficult

Joins to and from s

Remember: for diagonal joins to s, change to a shorter s.

Learning intention: To practise joins to and from s

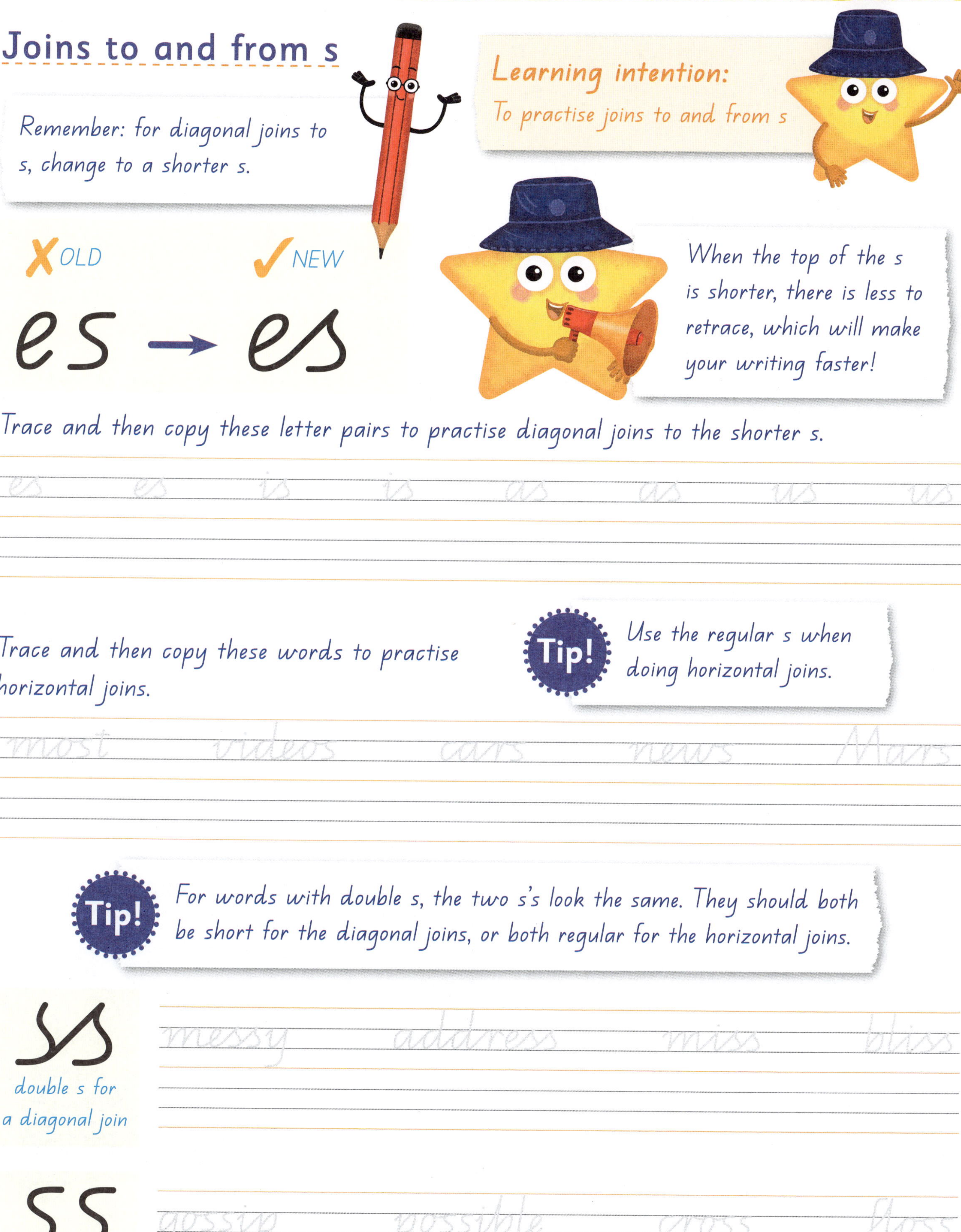

When the top of the s is shorter, there is less to retrace, which will make your writing faster!

Trace and then copy these letter pairs to practise diagonal joins to the shorter s.

es es is is as as us us

Trace and then copy these words to practise horizontal joins.

Tip! Use the regular s when doing horizontal joins.

most videos cars news Mars

Tip! For words with double s, the two s's look the same. They should both be short for the diagonal joins, or both regular for the horizontal joins.

ss
double s for a diagonal join

messy address miss bliss

ss
double s for a horizontal join

gossip possible cross floss

Joins to and from x

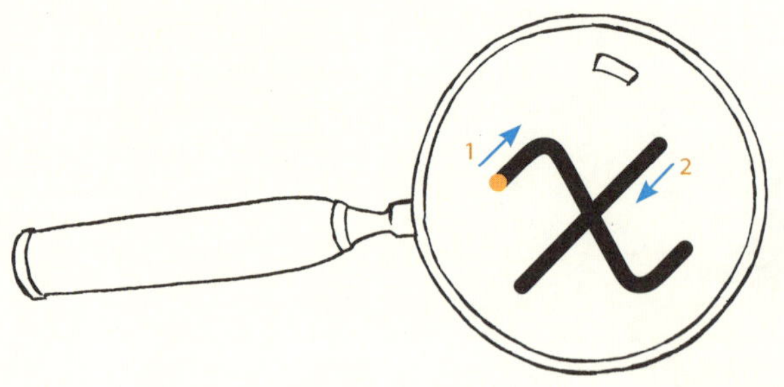

Tip! Take the join from the x high to the next letter, then cross the x.

Step 1
an

Step 2
ax

Step 3
axe

Trace and copy these words with joins to and from x.

explore fix mix box boxer

galaxy wax explosion exit

sixty mixer

text extreme

taxi explode

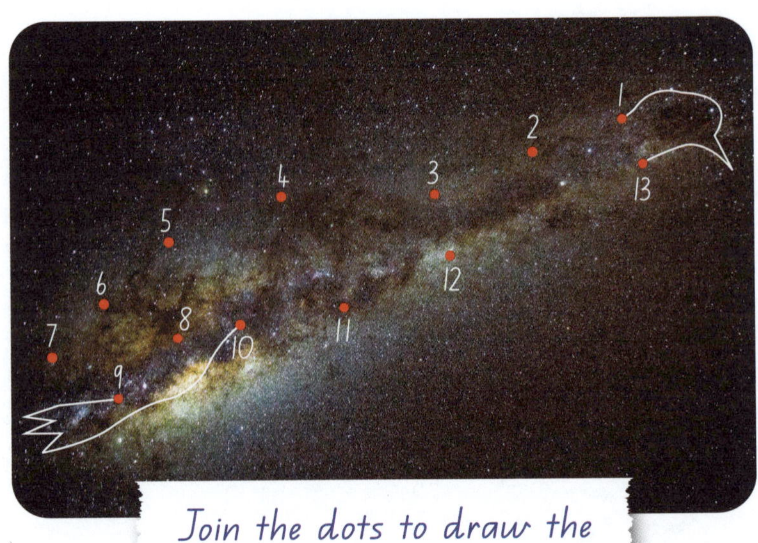

Join the dots to draw the Emu constellation, which is part of the Milky Way.

Letters that do not join

Introducing clockwise finishers

Learning intention:
To write letters that have clockwise finishers: b, g, j, p, s, y and z

Trace over the following letters. Draw a star to show where the letter ends. Draw an arrow to show the direction your pencil is heading in as you finish the letter. The first one is done for you.

b g j p s y z

Tip! Letters that finish in a clockwise direction do not join.

Trace and then copy these letters with clockwise finishers.

b g j p s y z b g j p s y z

be best bi biggest bo boy

ba back bu buying bl black

bu buzz bi billions be beyond

ga gas ga gallop ga gain

ge get gi digital go gone

Practising clockwise finishers

Trace and then copy these letter pairs and words.

Learning intention:
To practise writing letters with clockwise finishers

gh bought ju just jo jobs

ja jam ji jig pa past

pi picture pe people po pole

pl play sa said sh shopping

so solve sp spark su sunset

st slide st stayed si sister

so some yo you yu yum

ya yabby ye yellow yo young

za zap ze zero zi zigzag zo zoo

Learning intention: To practise writing the letter q

The letter q

The letter q does not join to the next letter.

Trace and then copy these letters.

q q q q q q

qu qu qu qu qu qu

Trace and then copy these words.

quiet quiz liquid quest quick quasar

Trace and then copy these sentences.

Kyah and Jazz live in 2125. When they are

on school holidays, they like to fly from pole

to pole until they get dizzy. They can zoom

quickly past mountains and then be back

home in time for a yummy dinner.

Capitals

Learning intention: To write capital letters

Trace and then copy these names.

Ananya Henry Alessia Moon Binh

Emma Sirius Adam Hoa Ethan

South Pole Nico Charlie Natalia

Answer these questions on the lines below.

In which month were you born?	In which country were you born?	On which planet were you born?

Draw a star on the world map to show where you were born.

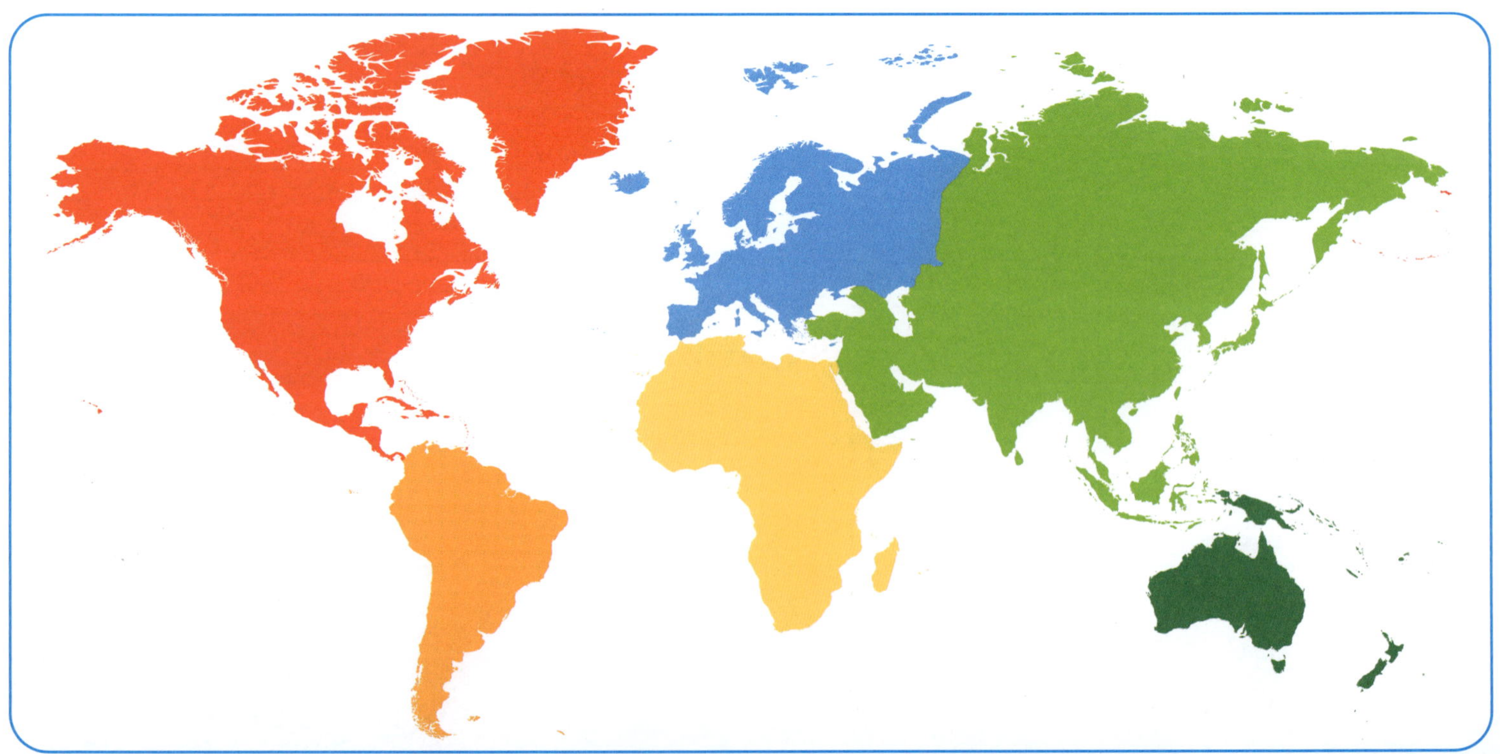

Assessment: Letters that do not join

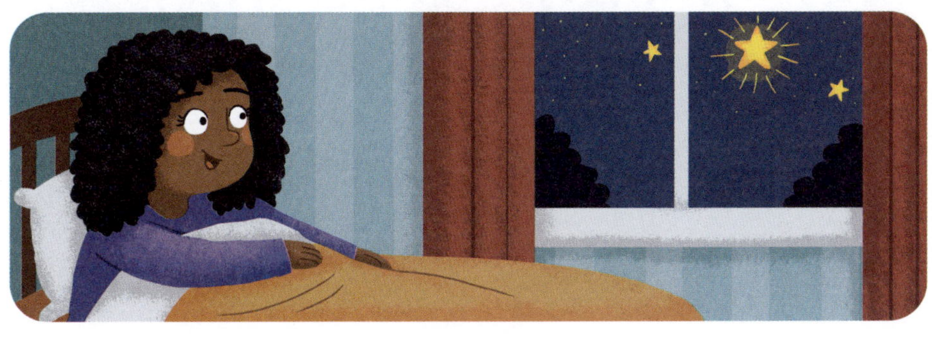

Capital letters do not join. Circle the letters that should be capitals, then rewrite the text correctly.

one night, juliette woke up quietly and

saw a bright light shining in the sky.

juliette knew it wasn't the morning but

then she remembered her teacher telling

her that sirius is the brightest star in

earth's night sky.

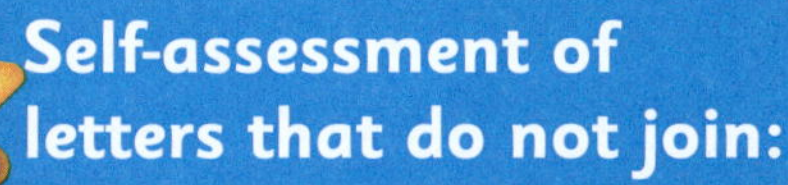

Self-assessment of letters that do not join:

Congratulations! You've learnt about letters that do not join. Colour in your progress on page 3.

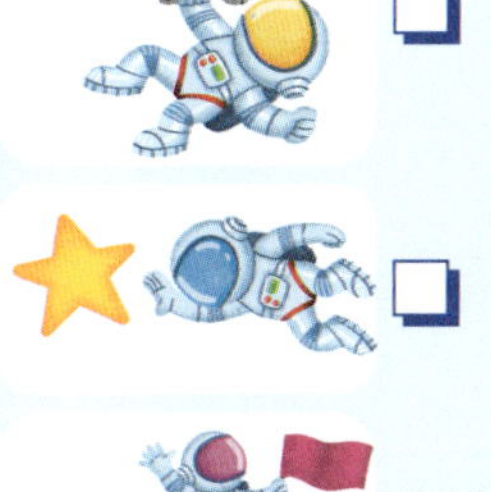

❑ *I need more confidence*

❑ *I understand but need practice*

❑ *Over the Moon!*

Teacher comment

Fluency and legibility

Practising cursive handwriting

Learning intention:
To practise cursive handwriting

Trace and then copy these sentences.

A star is a hot, glowing ball of gas. When

you look into the night sky, you can see

many shining stars, especially if you

are away from city lights. The light we

see in the daytime comes from the closest

star: the Sun. The Sun is approximately

150 million kilometres

from Earth.

Rewrite the information in these fact files in cursive handwriting.

Mars is red and is the fourth planet from the Sun.

Neptune is blue and is the eighth planet from the Sun.

Saturn has rings and is the sixth planet from the Sun.

The Kuiper belt has asteroids and dwarf planets.

Kuiper belt

Do you know how to pronounce Kuiper? You say KIGH-puh.

Size, slope and spacing

Rewrite the text, keeping in mind the size and slope of your writing.

Use your finger between words to make an even space.

The solar system is named after the Sun.

The word "sol" means sun in Latin.

All the planets in the solar system revolve around the Sun. Do you know the origin of the word "planet"? It comes from the Greek "planetes", which means "wanderer".

Continue the fluency pattern.

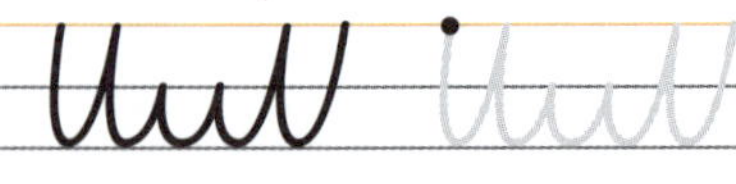

OXFORD UNIVERSITY PRESS

Numbers

Trace and then copy these numbers.

1 2 3 4 5 6 7 8 9 10

10 20 30 40 50 60 70 80 90 100

Write these numbers as words on each line. The first one is done for you.

11 eleven eleven eleven eleven

12 twelve

13 thirteen

14 fourteen

15 fifteen

16 sixteen

17 seventeen

18 eighteen

19 nineteen

20 twenty

21 twenty-one

Punctuation

Trace and then copy these punctuation marks and their names.

. . . full stop . . .

, , , comma , , ,

! ! ! exclamation mark ! ! !

? ? ? question mark ? ? ?

“ ” speech marks “ ”

Copy these sentences and choose the right punctuation mark to go in each sentence.

Space travel is amazing

Do you have a favourite planet

This is a great book, said the librarian

Labelling maps and diagrams

Complete the state and territory names on the map of Australia.

Learning intention:
Use print handwriting for labels

We use Queensland Beginner's print handwriting to label maps and diagrams.

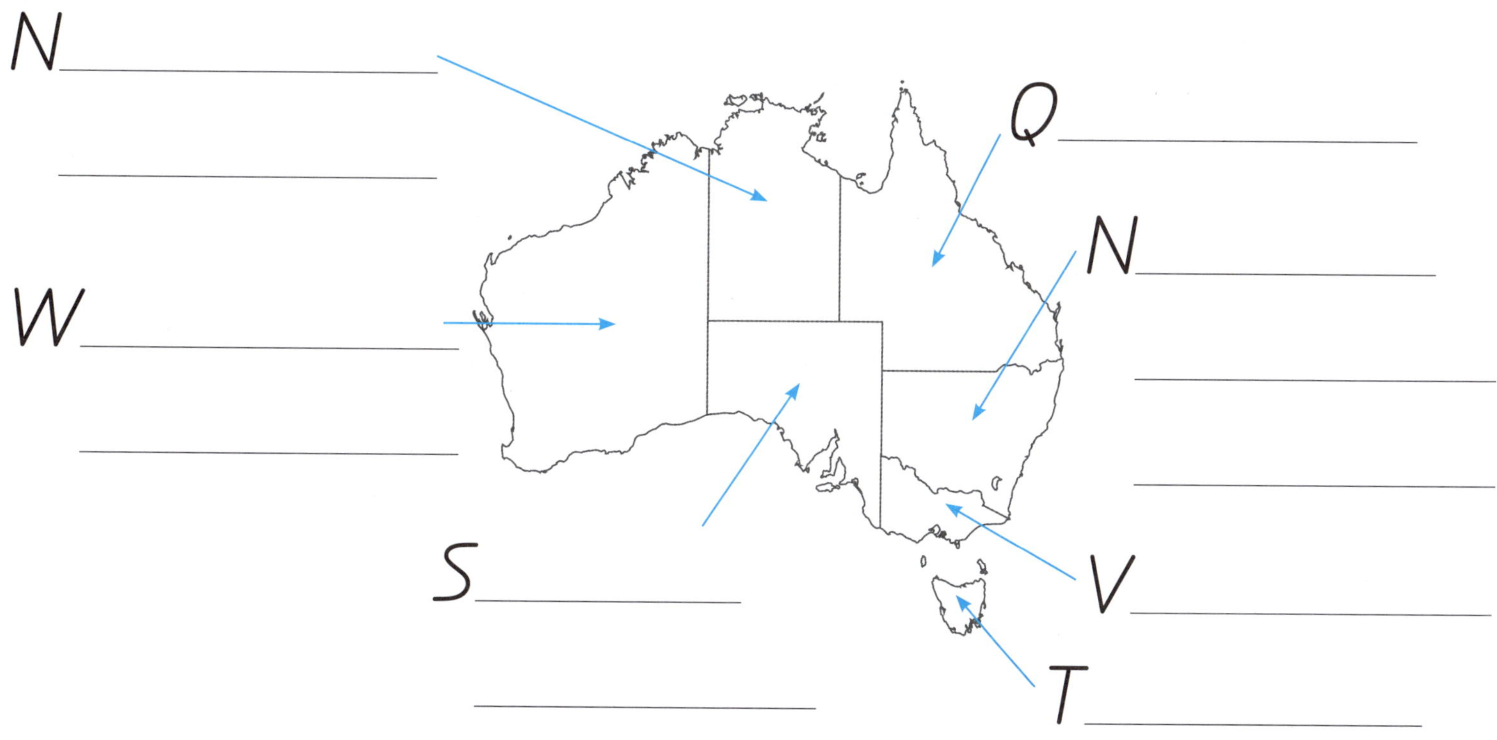

Label the planets in our solar system. Fill in the missing letters, using your knowledge from this book to help you.

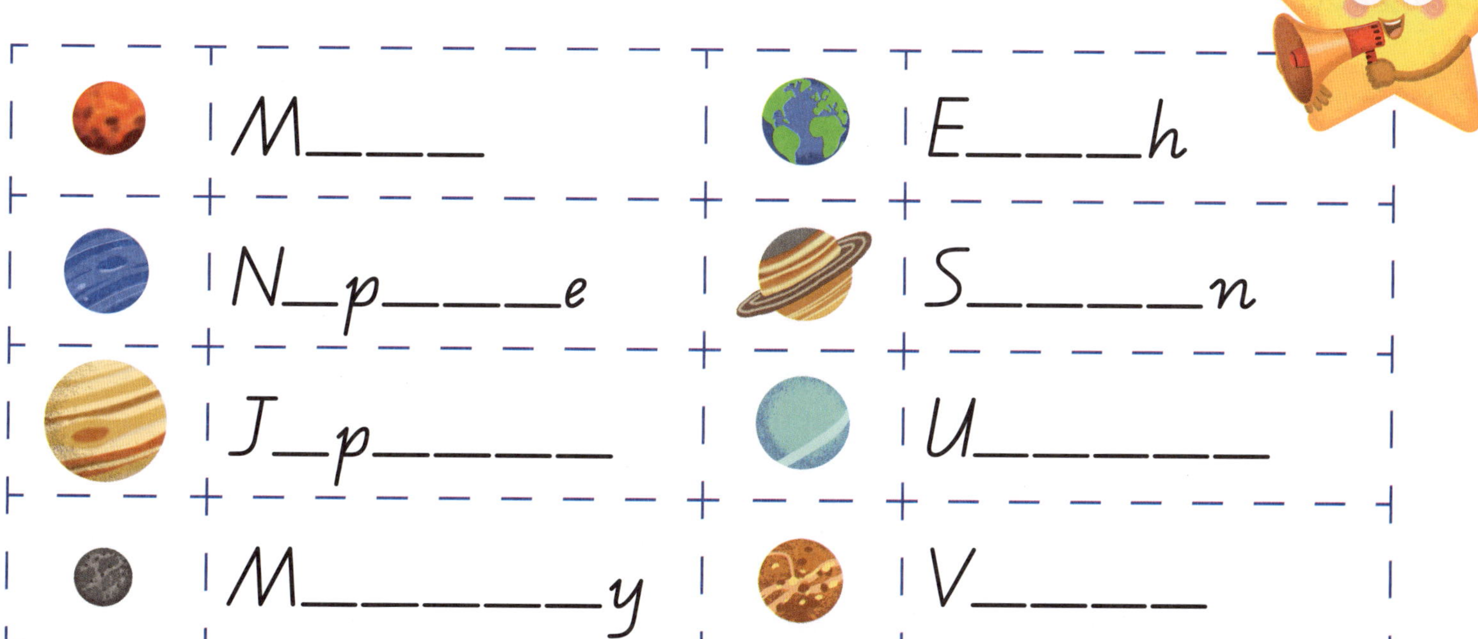

Building fluency

Practise writing these words three times each.

first

team

know

ride

time

amazing

fast

people

flying

watch

walking

awesome

beautiful

playground

swimming

animals

football

happily

morning

family

Word play

Complete the word search. Words can go upwards, downwards and across.
When you've found all the words, colour in the letters that are left over.

S	O	C	S	O	L	A	R	B	D	E	M	F
T	R	D	T	E	A	R	F	D	S	T	O	J
C	P	L	A	N	E	T	V	S	H	E	O	K
O	F	R	R	L	E	R	T	W	Q	S	N	Y
N	S	U	R	N	D	F	R	A	D	X	V	S
E	A	R	T	H	P	E	T	C	G	O	R	T
Q	T	R	I	N	G	S	Y	O	R	B	I	T
L	L	C	G	H	J	T	H	M	A	H	E	S
R	O	C	K	E	T	F	S	E	V	N	B	S
V	R	E	S	R	T	W	F	T	I	H	T	U
C	O	N	S	T	E	L	L	A	T	I	O	N
O	P	B	D	S	S	C	O	N	Y	R	I	N

solar star planet constellation gravity
orbit Earth Sun Moon rings rocket comet

Independent writing

Choose a planet to conduct some research on. On the next page, complete the fact file on your planet.

Print the name of your planet.

Draw your planet.

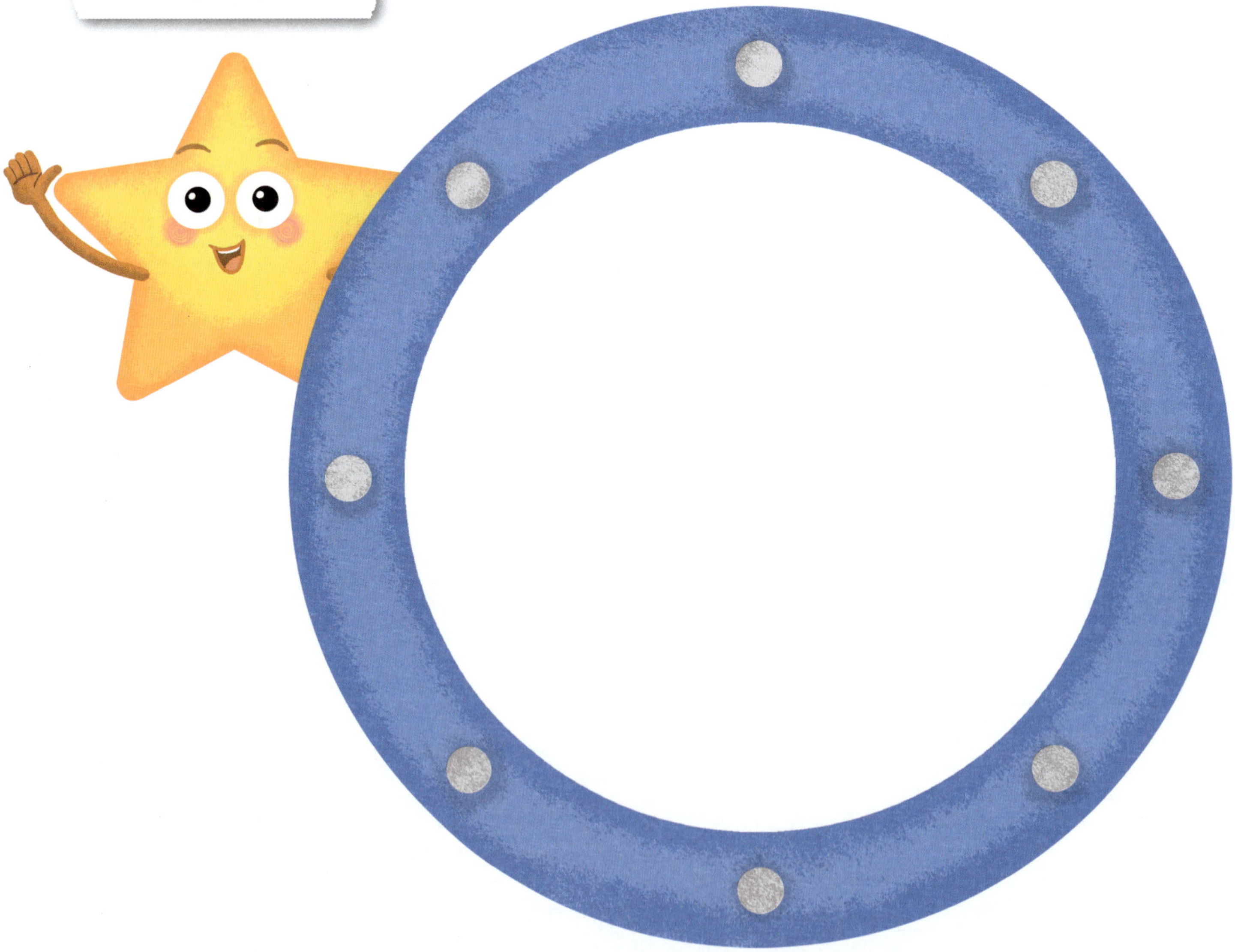

My planet fact file

Assessment: Fluency and legibility

Copy these sentences in your best cursive handwriting.

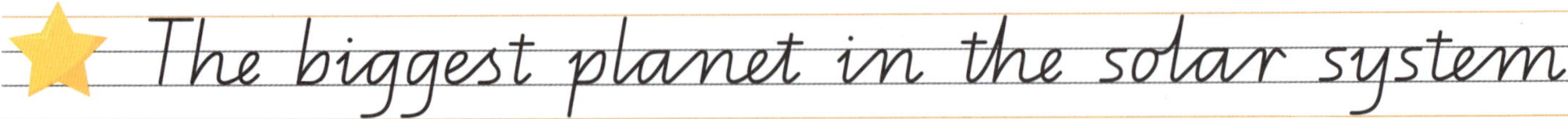

is Jupiter. Jupiter is twice as massive

as all the other planets combined.

to complete an orbit of the Sun.

Self-assessment of fluency and legibility:

Congratulations! You've learnt how to write legibly and with fluency. Go to page 3 to complete your passport.

❏ I need more confidence

❏ I understand but need practice

❏ Over the Moon!

I hope you had fun and improved your writing on this journey.

Teacher comment